He Has MADE EVERYTHING Beautiful IN ITS TIME

ECCLESIASTES 3:11

Prayer Journal

ASHLEY BENJAMIN

Copyright © 2019 by Ashley M. Benjamin

All rights reserved. No part of this book may be reproduced or used in any manner without written permission of the copyright owner except for the use of quotations in a book review.

For more information, email:

hello@brownshuggah.com

FIRST EDITION

www.brownshuggah.com

This Prayer Journal Belongs to:

Prayers for My Family

DATE   NAME

Be Still and Know That I'm With You...
Psalm 46:10

Prayers for Myself

DATE REFLECTIONS

Prayers For My Friends

DATE   NAMES

For with God, nothing is impossible...

Prayers For my loves

DATE NAME

My Prayer

DATE / /

Prayer JOURNAL

PERSONAL REFLECTIONS

Spiritual Inspiration

" I can do All THINGS through CHRIST WHO STRENGTHENS ME "

- PHILIPPIANS 4:13 -

DATE / /

Sermon JOURNAL

WHAT I LEARNED TODAY

Notes:

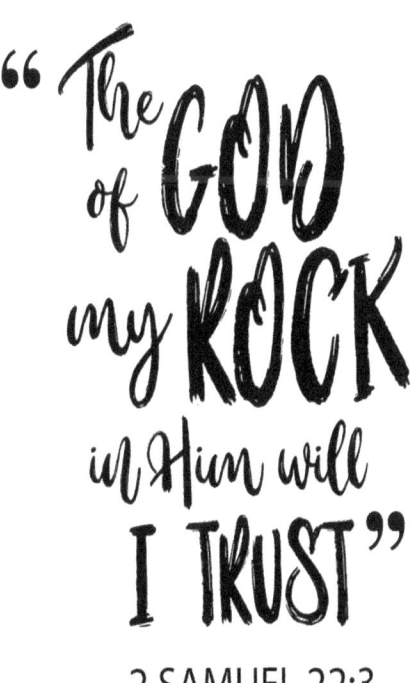

"The God of my ROCK in Him will I TRUST"

- 2 SAMUEL 22:3 -

DATE / /

Sermon JOURNAL

WHAT I LEARNED TODAY

𝒩otes:

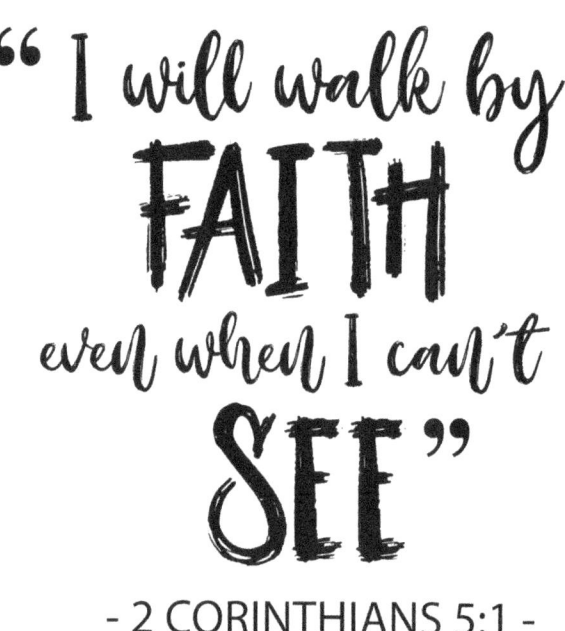

DATE / /

Sermon JOURNAL

WHAT I LEARNED TODAY

Notes:

"Be Still in the Presence of the LORD and wait patiently for him to act."

- PSALM 37:7 -

DATE / /

Sermon JOURNAL

WHAT I LEARNED TODAY

Notes:

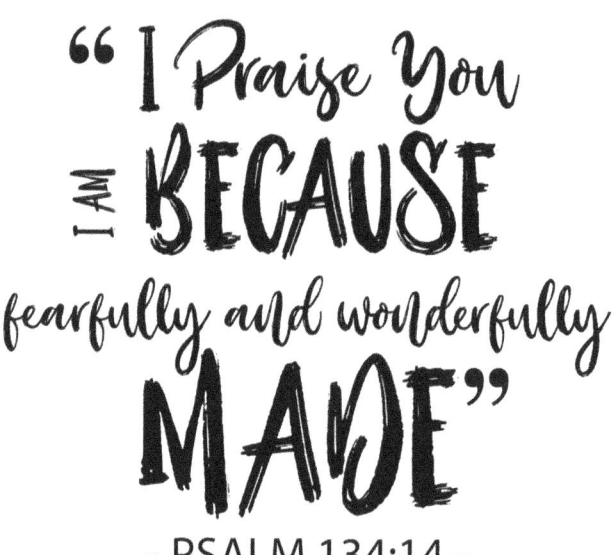

"I Praise You BECAUSE I AM fearfully and wonderfully MADE"

- PSALM 134:14 -

DATE / /

Sermon JOURNAL

WHAT I LEARNED TODAY

Notes:

"Be Not Afraid, only BELIEVE"
- MARK 5:36 -

I AM GRATEFUL FOR

DATE / /

Sermon JOURNAL

WHAT I LEARNED TODAY

Notes:

"By his wounds we are HEALED"
- ISAIAH 53:5 -

I AM GRATEFUL FOR

Prayer Requests

DATE　　　　　　　　　　　　　　NAMES

Prayer Card　　　　　　　　　　　Prayer Card

Hymn Study

HYMN:

Favorite Verse

Lyrics of Faith

Sing to him, Sing praise to him, tell of all his wonderful acts.
Psalm 105:2

Sermon NOTES

DATE / /   TOPIC:

SPEAKER: PLACE OF WORSHIP:

SCRIPTURE   NOTES

Key Points

sermon TRACKER

DATE

SCRIPTURE

NOTES

Reflections

DATE

Today's stand-out verse:

I am thankful for:

Prayer Requests:

Inspirational Scripture:

Sermon NOTES

DATE / / TOPIC

Scripture

Prayer & Praise

Personal Reflections

Sermon NOTES

DATE

SERMON

Scripture

Notes

Be on your guard; stand firm in the faith; be courageous; be strong.
1 Corinthians 4:16-18

Sermon NOTES

DATE / /   TOPIC:

SPEAKER: PLACE OF WORSHIP:

Key Points

In GOD we trust

DATE:

This week I will focus on:

What I am most grateful for:

In **GOD** *we trust*

DATE:

This week I was most blessed by:

My calling in life is:

In **GOD** we trust

DATE:

My favorite passage of scripture is:

God is leading me to make the following changes:

In **GOD** we trust

DATE:

I feel God's presence most when:

What brings me the most joy is:

In **GOD** *we trust*

DATE:

My spiritual gifts are:

My enthusiasm for the gospel is increased when:

*In **GOD** we trust*

DATE:

One way I can apply the gospel to my life is:

An act of obedience God is prompting me to take is:

My time with the LORD

DATE:

Scripture that inspired me today:

Dear Lord:

Prayers for My Family

DATE　　　　　　　　　　　NAME

Be Still and Know That I'm With You...
Psalm 46:10

Prayers for Myself

DATE   REFLECTIONS

Prayers For My Friends

DATE — NAMES

For with God, nothing is impossible...

Prayers For my loves

DATE   NAME

My Prayer

DATE / /

Prayer JOURNAL

PERSONAL REFLECTIONS

Spiritual Inspiration

"**I can do All THINGS through CHRIST WHO STRENGTHENS ME**"

- PHILIPPIANS 4:13 -

DATE / /

Sermon JOURNAL

WHAT I LEARNED TODAY

Notes:

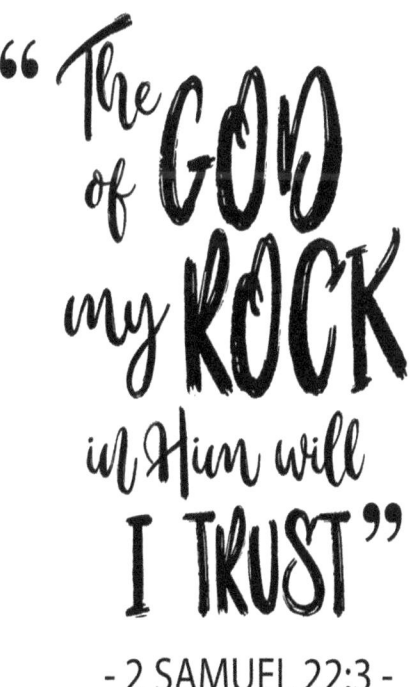

- 2 SAMUEL 22:3 -

DATE / /

Sermon JOURNAL

WHAT I LEARNED TODAY

Notes:

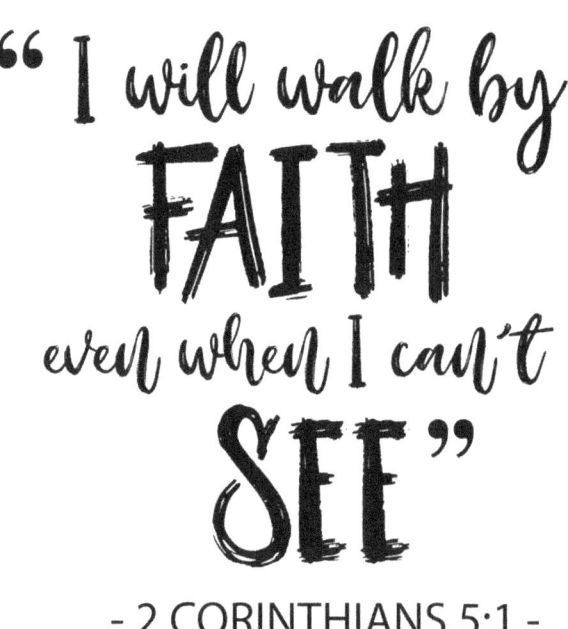

"I will walk by FAITH even when I can't SEE"

- 2 CORINTHIANS 5:1 -

DATE / /

Sermon JOURNAL

WHAT I LEARNED TODAY

Notes:

"*Be Still in the Presence of the* **LORD** *and wait patiently for him to act.*"

- PSALM 37:7 -

DATE / /

Sermon JOURNAL

WHAT I LEARNED TODAY

Notes:

" I Praise You
I AM **BECAUSE**
fearfully and wonderfully
MADE "

- PSALM 134:14 -

DATE / /

Sermon JOURNAL

WHAT I LEARNED TODAY

Notes:

"Be Not Afraid, only BELIEVE"
- MARK 5:36 -

I AM GRATEFUL FOR

DATE / /

Sermon JOURNAL

WHAT I LEARNED TODAY

Notes:

"By his wounds we are HEALED"
- ISAIAH 53:5 -

I AM GRATEFUL FOR

Prayer Requests

DATE   NAMES

Prayer Card   *Prayer Card*

Hymn Study

HYMN:

Favorite Verse

Lyrics of Faith

Sing to him, Sing praise to him, tell of all his wonderful acts.
Psalm 105:2

Sermon NOTES

DATE / / TOPIC:

SPEAKER: PLACE OF WORSHIP:

SCRIPTURE NOTES

Key Points

sermon TRACKER

DATE

SCRIPTURE

NOTES

Reflections

DATE

Today's stand-out verse:　　　*I am thankful for:*

Prayer Requests:　　　*Inspirational Scripture:*

Sermon NOTES

DATE / /   TOPIC

Scripture

Prayer & Praise

Personal Reflections

Sermon NOTES

DATE

SERMON

Scripture

Notes

Be on your guard; stand firm in the faith; be courageous; be strong.
1 Corinthians 4:16-18

Sermon NOTES

DATE / /   TOPIC:

SPEAKER: PLACE OF WORSHIP:

Key Points

In **GOD** *we trust*

DATE:

This week I will focus on:

What I am most grateful for:

In **GOD** *we trust*

DATE:

This week I was most blessed by:

My calling in life is:

In **GOD** we trust

DATE:

My favorite passage of scripture is:

God is leading me to make the following changes:

"He gives me
STRENGTH
when I'm
weak"

Prayers for My Family

DATE   NAME

Be Still and Know That I'm With You...
Psalm 46:10

Prayers for Myself

DATE | REFLECTIONS

Prayers For My Friends

DATE   NAMES

For with God, nothing is impossible...

Prayers For my loves

DATE   NAME

My Prayer

DATE / /

Prayer JOURNAL

PERSONAL REFLECTIONS

Spiritual Inspiration

" I can do All THINGS through CHRIST WHO STRENGTHENS ME "

- PHILIPPIANS 4:13 -

DATE / /

Sermon JOURNAL

WHAT I LEARNED TODAY

Notes:

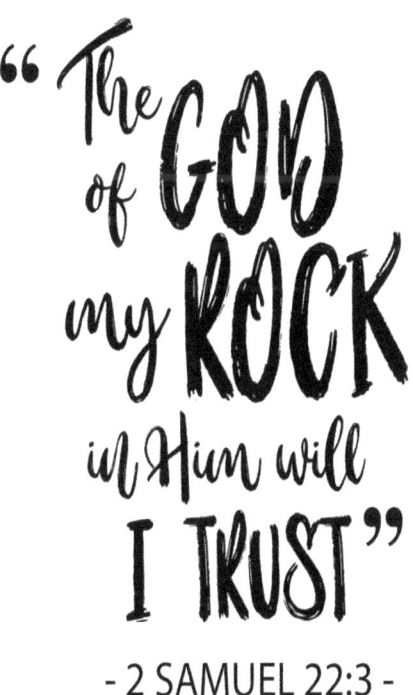

"The God of my ROCK in Him will I TRUST"

- 2 SAMUEL 22:3 -

DATE / /

Sermon JOURNAL

WHAT I LEARNED TODAY

Notes:

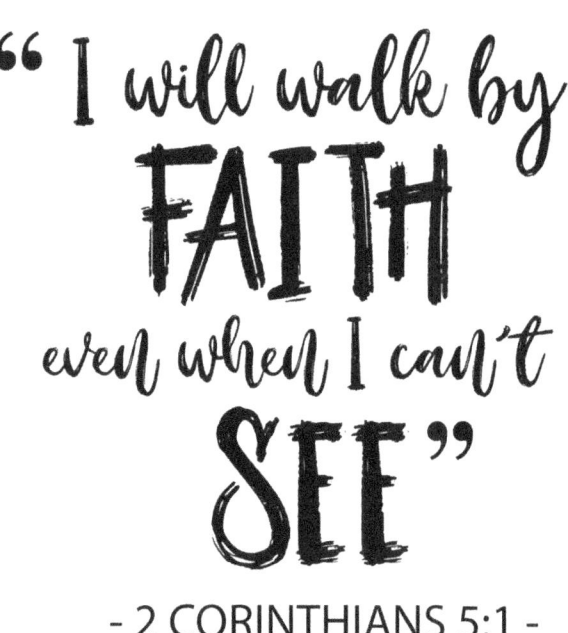

"I will walk by FAITH even when I can't SEE"

- 2 CORINTHIANS 5:1 -

DATE / /

Sermon JOURNAL

WHAT I LEARNED TODAY

Notes:

"Be Still in the Presence of the LORD and wait patiently for him to act."

- PSALM 37:7 -

DATE / /

Sermon JOURNAL

WHAT I LEARNED TODAY

Notes:

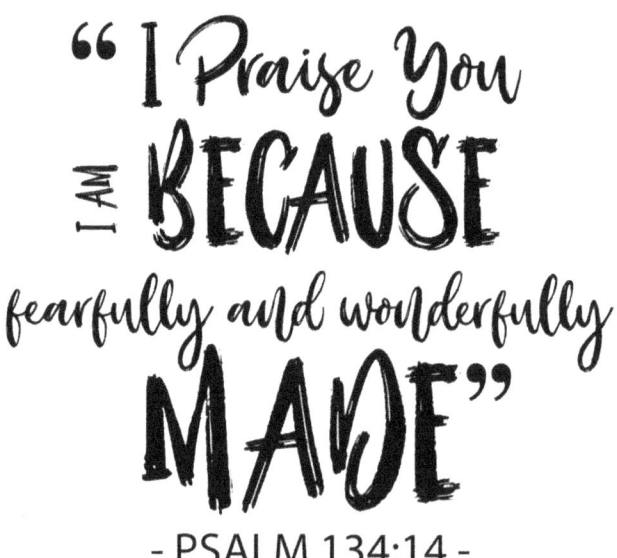

"I Praise You
because
I AM
fearfully and wonderfully
MADE"

- PSALM 134:14 -

DATE / /

Sermon JOURNAL

WHAT I LEARNED TODAY

Notes:

"Be Not Afraid, only BELIEVE"
- MARK 5:36 -

I AM GRATEFUL FOR

DATE / /

Sermon JOURNAL

WHAT I LEARNED TODAY

Notes:

"By his wounds we are HEALED"
- ISAIAH 53:5 -

I AM GRATEFUL FOR

Prayer Requests

DATE NAMES

Prayer Card *Prayer Card*

Hymn Study

HYMN:

Favorite Verse

Lyrics of Faith

Sing to him, Sing praise to him, tell of all his wonderful acts.
Psalm 105:2

Sermon NOTES

DATE / /   TOPIC:

SPEAKER: PLACE OF WORSHIP:

SCRIPTURE   NOTES

Key Points

sermon TRACKER

DATE

SCRIPTURE

NOTES

Reflections

DATE

Today's stand-out verse:

I am thankful for:

Prayer Requests:

Inspirational Scripture:

Sermon NOTES

DATE / /   TOPIC

Scripture

Prayer & Praise

Personal Reflections

Sermon NOTES

DATE

SERMON

Scripture

Notes

Be on your guard; stand firm in the faith; be courageous; be strong.
1 Corinthians 4:16-18

Sermon NOTES

DATE / /   TOPIC:

SPEAKER: PLACE OF WORSHIP:

Key Points

In **GOD** *we trust*

DATE:

This week I will focus on:

What I am most grateful for:

In **GOD** *we trust*

DATE:

This week I was most blessed by:

My calling in life is:

In **GOD** we trust

DATE:

My favorite passage of scripture is:

God is leading me to make the following changes:

"Life-long SIKTNGTH..."

Prayers for My Family

DATE   NAME

Be Still and Know That I'm With You...
Psalm 46:10

Prayers for Myself

DATE   REFLECTIONS

Prayers For My Friends

DATE NAMES

For with God, nothing is impossible...

Prayers For my loves

DATE   NAME

My Prayer

DATE / /

Prayer JOURNAL

PERSONAL REFLECTIONS

Spiritual Inspiration

"I can do All THINGS through CHRIST WHO STRENGTHENS ME"

- PHILIPPIANS 4:13 -

DATE / /

Sermon JOURNAL

WHAT I LEARNED TODAY

$\mathcal{N}otes:$

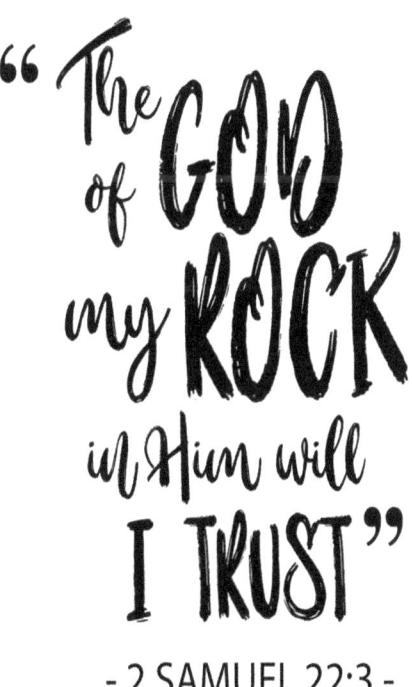

"The God of my Rock in Him will I trust"

- 2 SAMUEL 22:3 -

DATE / /

Sermon JOURNAL

WHAT I LEARNED TODAY

Notes:

" I will walk by **FAITH** even when I can't **SEE** "

- 2 CORINTHIANS 5:1 -

DATE / /

Sermon JOURNAL

WHAT I LEARNED TODAY

Notes:

> "Be Still in the Presence of the LORD and wait patiently for him to act."
> — PSALM 37:7 —

DATE / /

Sermon JOURNAL

WHAT I LEARNED TODAY

Notes:

"I Praise You BECAUSE I AM fearfully and wonderfully MADE"

- PSALM 134:14 -

DATE / /

Sermon JOURNAL

WHAT I LEARNED TODAY

Notes:

"Be Not Afraid, only BELIEVE"
- MARK 5:36 -

I AM GRATEFUL FOR

DATE / /

Sermon JOURNAL

WHAT I LEARNED TODAY

Notes:

"By his wounds we are HEALED"
- ISAIAH 53:5 -

I AM GRATEFUL FOR

Prayer Requests

DATE   NAMES

Prayer Card   *Prayer Card*

Hymn Study

HYMN:

Favorite Verse

Lyrics of Faith

Sing to him, Sing praise to him, tell of all his wonderful acts.
Psalm 105:2

Sermon NOTES

DATE / /   TOPIC:

SPEAKER: PLACE OF WORSHIP:

SCRIPTURE   NOTES

Key Points

sermon TRACKER

DATE

SCRIPTURE

NOTES

Reflections

DATE

Today's stand-out verse: *I am thankful for:*

Prayer Requests: *Inspirational Scripture:*

Sermon NOTES

DATE / /   TOPIC

Scripture

Prayer & Praise

Personal Reflections

Sermon NOTES

DATE

SERMON

Scripture

Notes

Be on your guard; stand firm in the faith; be courageous; be strong.
1 Corinthians 4:16-18

Sermon NOTES

DATE / /   TOPIC:

SPEAKER: PLACE OF WORSHIP:

Key Points

In **GOD** *we trust*

DATE:

This week I will focus on:

What I am most grateful for:

*In **GOD** we trust*

DATE:

This week I was most blessed by:

My calling in life is:

In **GOD** *we trust*

DATE:

My favorite passage of scripture is:

God is leading me to make the following changes:

"Not by my STRENGTH by HIS"

Prayers for My Family

DATE NAME

Be Still and Know That I'm With You...
Psalm 46:10

Prayers for Myself

DATE REFLECTIONS

Prayers For My Friends

DATE   NAMES

For with God, nothing is impossible...

Prayers For my loves

DATE NAME

My Prayer

DATE / /

Prayer JOURNAL

PERSONAL REFLECTIONS

Spiritual Inspiration

" **I can do All THINGS** *through* **CHRIST** WHO STRENGTHENS ME "

- PHILIPPIANS 4:13 -

DATE / /

Sermon JOURNAL

WHAT I LEARNED TODAY

Notes:

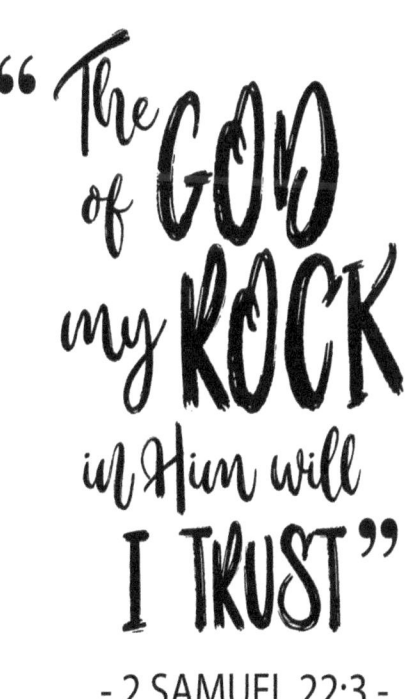

"The God of my Rock in Him will I Trust"

- 2 SAMUEL 22:3 -

DATE / /

Sermon JOURNAL

WHAT I LEARNED TODAY

Notes:

> "I will walk by **FAITH** even when I can't **SEE**"
>
> - 2 CORINTHIANS 5:1 -

DATE / /

Sermon JOURNAL

WHAT I LEARNED TODAY

Notes:

> "Be Still in the Presence of the LORD and wait patiently for him to act."
> — PSALM 37:7 —

DATE / /

Sermon JOURNAL

WHAT I LEARNED TODAY

Notes:

"I Praise You BECAUSE I AM fearfully and wonderfully MADE"

- PSALM 134:14 -

DATE / /

Sermon JOURNAL

WHAT I LEARNED TODAY

Notes:

"Be Not Afraid, only BELIEVE"
- MARK 5:36 -

I AM GRATEFUL FOR

DATE / /

Sermon JOURNAL

WHAT I LEARNED TODAY

Notes:

"By his wounds we are HEALED"
- ISAIAH 53:5 -

I AM GRATEFUL FOR

Prayer Requests

DATE   NAMES

Prayer Card   Prayer Card

Hymn Study

HYMN:

Favorite Verse

Lyrics of Faith

Sing to him, Sing praise to him, tell of all his wonderful acts.
Psalm 105:2

Sermon NOTES

DATE / /   TOPIC:

SPEAKER: PLACE OF WORSHIP:

SCRIPTURE   NOTES

Key Points

sermon TRACKER

DATE

SCRIPTURE

NOTES

Reflections

DATE

Today's stand-out verse: *I am thankful for:*

Prayer Requests: *Inspirational Scripture:*

Sermon NOTES

DATE / /   TOPIC

Scripture

Prayer & Praise

Personal Reflections

Sermon NOTES

DATE

SERMON

Scripture

Notes

Be on your guard; stand firm in the faith; be courageous; be strong.
1 Corinthians 4:16-18

Sermon NOTES

DATE / /   TOPIC:

SPEAKER: PLACE OF WORSHIP:

Key Points

DATE / /

Sermon JOURNAL

WHAT I LEARNED TODAY

Notes:

" I will walk by **FAITH** even when I can't **SEE** "

- 2 CORINTHIANS 5:1 -

www.ingramcontent.com/pod-product-compliance
Lightning Source LLC
Chambersburg PA
CBHW080454170426
43196CB00016B/2795